HERE AND NOW

An Interactive Mindfulness Book

FERN TAYLOR

Thorsons

Thorsons
An imprint of HarperCollins*Publishers*
1 London Bridge Street
London SE1 9GF

www.harpercollins.co.uk

First published by HarperCollins*Publishers* 2017

10 9 8 7 6 5 4 3 2 1

A catalogue record of this book is available from the British Library

ISBN 978-0-00-821658-0

Printed and bound in China

MIX
Paper from
responsible sources
FSC® C007454

FSC™ is a non-profit international organisation established to promote
the responsible management of the world's forests. Products carrying the
FSC label are independently certified to assure consumers that they come
from forests that are managed to meet the social, economic and ecological
needs of present and future generations, and other controlled sources.

Find out more about HarperCollins and the environment at
www.harpercollins.co.uk/green

SOUND BUTTON

Press this button to become aware of all the sounds
around you and the silences between the sounds.

CONTENTS

INTRODUCTION

YOU ARE HERE.
YOU ARE UNIQUE.

You can use these activities in any order, at any time, in whatever way feels right for you.

Each activity opens up a space in which you may begin to explore the present moment in and around you. There are no right or wrong responses. Try to approach each activity without expectation. Simply notice your experience, whatever it is.

You can 'dip in' and choose an activity that feels right for you or you can work your way through from start to finish. Spend as long as you like on each activity – there are no rules.

Be curious, be playful and experiment. Most importantly, have fun and enjoy discovering the here and now!

USING THESE ACTIVITIES IN YOUR DAILY LIFE

You can come back to these activities again and again. Even when you are familiar with an activity, each time you try it will be a new and different experience. Try to approach the activities with a spirit of friendly curiosity.

Over time, you may notice that some activities are particularly helpful at a certain time of day or when you are experiencing a certain emotion. You might note these observations down in a journal or on the page to help you come back to them again when needed.

Perhaps you could carry this book with you so you can use the activities whenever you need a moment of calm. In the midst of a busy day, even a short break in which to breathe and come back to the present moment can be very beneficial.

You could experiment with setting a routine for your practice. Maybe you could do five minutes in the morning before you start your day, or in the evening before you go to bed. Remember, there is no 'right' way to be mindful. Try to let go of what you think you 'should' be doing and enjoy whatever works for you.

Have fun! Playing with different approaches and noticing how they make you feel is a great mindfulness practice in itself.

TURN THE PAGE & BEGIN!

BODY SCAN

Run your fingertip over the body.

As your finger touches the page it will connect with any sensations in that part of your physical body.

Slowly scan your body. Notice how different parts of your body feel. How do your muscles feel? Which places are more tense than others?

Gently release any tension you feel.

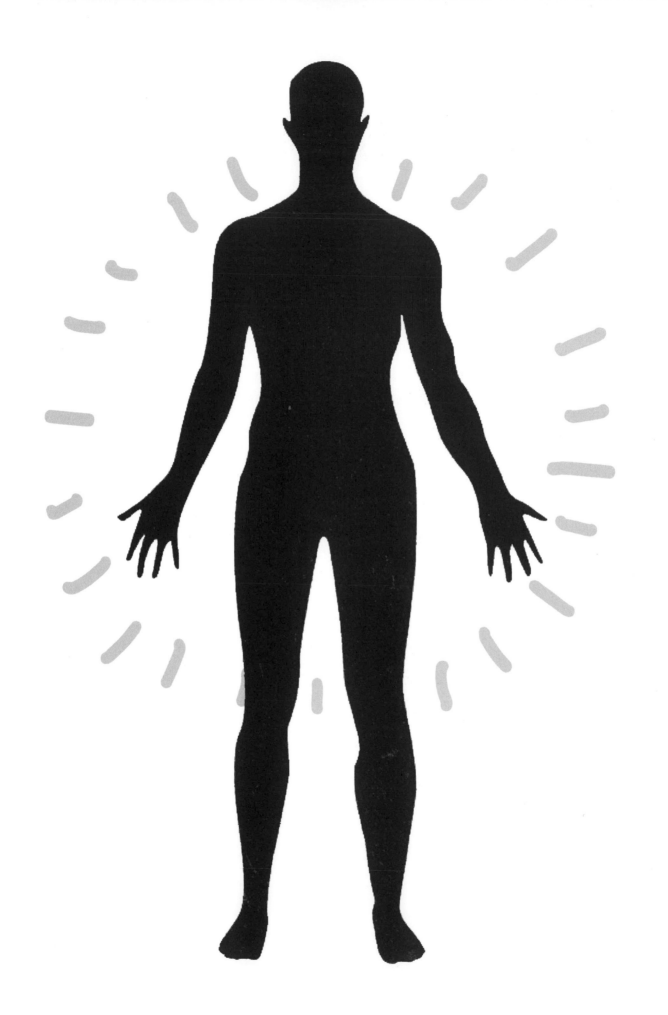

5

TOUCHING SPACE

On the page opposite, draw around your hand. Remove your hand.

Now, focus your attention on the space where your hand was. Feel into the space, the memory of sensation, the presence of imprint.

Look around you at the space in which you exist right now. Put your hand in five different places in the space around you, moving slowly between each position. You may choose to touch the air or something solid.

Keep in your mind a sense of these five touches. Be aware of the imprints and interactions your hand has made. Imagine a thread linking all of your handprints.

As you move around today, be aware of the sensations you feel in your hands and the handprints you leave.

A MOMENT TO PAUSE

The water in the jar on the page opposite is full of mud and impurities. Put your finger on the page and give the water a stir. Then pick up the book and give it a good shake to mix up the water and mud nicely.

Now, come back to your breath. Sit for twelve breaths, paying attention to the breath but not trying to change it. It may help to close your eyes. If your mind wanders, notice where it has wandered to, then come back to the breath.

Next, open your eyes and turn the page.

OPEN YOUR EYES & TURN THE PAGE

A MOMENT TO PAUSE

Notice how the water has changed . . .

In time, when the jar is still, all impurities naturally sink to the bottom and the water becomes calm and clear.

In the same way, you can calm your mind at any time by coming back to your breath.

BREATH

Place your finger on one of the outer circles. Become aware of your breath. Allow one complete in-breath and out-breath before moving your finger on to the next circle.

Each time you move your finger to the next circle, let the touch of your finger on the paper be a reminder to stay with the breath with quiet concentration.

For each breath, notice where the air touches your nostrils on the in-breath and the sensation as it moves into your body. Feel your lungs expand and your abdomen extend gently. Notice the pause between in-breath and out-breath. Feel your lungs and abdomen relax and fall as the breath begins to move out. Sense the breath on your upper lip as you exhale.

Watch your breath with gentle curiosity for the full duration of the in-breath and out-breath. There is no need to try to control or change it in any way. Simply be with it as it is.

If you get a desire to 'hurry' to complete the circle, simply come back to the feeling of your finger on the page and the sensation of your breath moving in and out of your body. Allow your breath to take the time that it takes and enjoy the softness of the movement. Know that by taking the time to be with your breath you are calming your nervous system and balancing your mind and body.

Now, place your finger on the middle circle and close your eyes. Enjoy three complete breaths before opening your eyes.

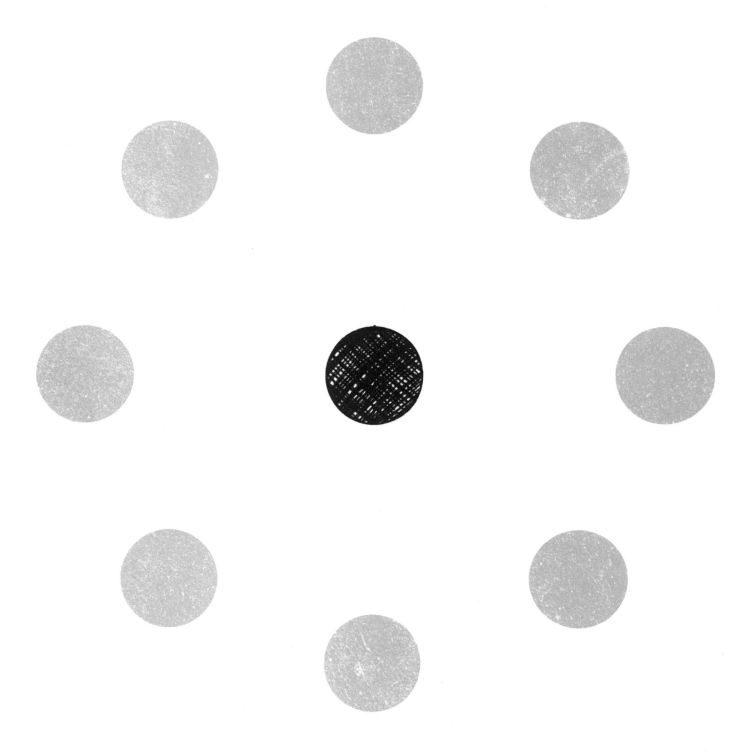

13

ENTER. SPACE. SHIFT.

Using the keyboard on the page opposite, type out any worry that you may have. Name what is there as honestly and precisely as you can. Use as many or as few words as you need. To acknowledge your worry, press ENTER . After pressing ENTER, pause for a moment. Use this time to check in with your body while your worry is registered.

Now, press SPACE . The space bar function opens up your awareness of the infinitely vast space around your worry. This process usually takes about three calm breaths. You may begin to notice the space around you with more awareness. You may feel your mind expand and reach out in any or all directions to the blue sky and universe beyond. Stay with this sense of space as long as feels comfortable.

Finally, the SHIFT function will bring your attention back to the feel of your feet touching the ground, your body resting on the chair or wherever you are, back to your breath and back to a feeling of calm. You can use this button at any time.

15

TOUCH THE EARTH

Place the book on the ground. Stand with your two feet flat on the page. Become aware of the earth beneath you. Notice any tension in your body and allow it to flow out into the earth. Feel how the earth is always there to support you.

For the rest of the day, be aware of the touch of your feet on the ground. Feel the soles of your feet caress the earth with each step you take.

TOUCH SCREEN EMOTION CIRCLES

Use your thumb and forefinger to **stretch** your chosen emotion outwards into a larger circle. This will allow whatever emotion you are feeling to really be seen. Watch it expand. What does it look like? What colours and shapes do you see? Where do you feel the emotion in your body? Notice how it feels.

Give your emotion as much time as it needs. Hold the space open and allow the emotion to be present. Allow it to be there as it is without trying to change it.

As you close the emotion by dragging the circle back into a small dot, notice the touch of your thumb and forefinger as they come back together. Focus for a moment on the feelings in your thumb and finger.

Thank yourself for giving your emotions time and space.

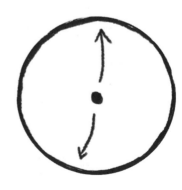

COMPASSION

SADNESS

FEAR

JOY

ANGER

[ANY OTHER
EMOTION]

BREATHE*NAME* RELEASE

Sit quietly. Allow yourself to breathe in and out quietly for ten breaths. Focus on the clear white box in the centre, allowing your mind to be spacious and at ease, allowing your breath to clear and calm your mind.

As you sit quietly and enjoy the space, thoughts and images may arise. This is natural: do not try to stop them.

Each time a thought arises, calmly swipe it across the page, bringing it into the large box so you can see it clearly and in colour. Quietly name the thought. You might say, 'This is a thought about food/thinking/pain/work,' or whatever comes up. Just acknowledge it.

There is no need to 'select', 'zoom in' or 'expand' a thought. You can thank your mind for producing the thought but you do not need to follow it. Now, simply swipe across the page again to release the thought. Your thought may still be present but it is no longer in the centre: you have returned to the clear white box once more. Focus on your breath again and continue for as long as feels comfortable.

Repeat this process of breathing, naming and letting go whenever you feel tense. Every time the ribbon of your mind gets gathered and tightly tied around you, you can breathe fully and with deep acceptance so that it loosens and opens again.

As your mind learns to trust that each thought will be seen, acknowledged and released, it will begin to loosen and feel free more and more of the time.

HOME PAGE

This is your home page. It is always here.

As spacious as the sky. As generous as the ocean.

A place to pause, to breathe, to rest.

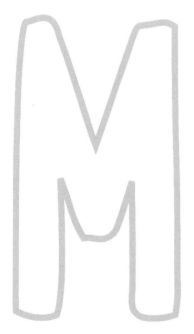 

 Press to unlock your mind and body.

Feel into the blank space, swim through the white page,

dissolve into the spaciousness. Rest.

+COMPASSION CHARGER+

+ Place your hand in the compassion charger. Feel a gentle smile in your eyes. Bring to mind the face of a loved one (human, animal or plant!). Allow thoughts of kindness towards this being to grow and spread through you. Feel your body soften as you sit with kindness. Try not to attach your thoughts to actions or specific outcomes but imagine your compassion as a warm glow that will envelop your loved one and soothe, comfort and nourish in whatever way is needed. Quietly say the compassion mantra as you focus on your loved one.

++ Now, bring the focus of your compassionate attention to yourself. This may be difficult at first — do not worry. It is enough to simply set the intention to feel compassion for yourself. Try to sit without judgement and acknowledge that you too have pain, vulnerability, seeds of joy and many good qualities. Gently repeat the compassion mantra for yourself, recognising how it feels to receive these words. You may notice compassion flow into you and fill you up from the top of your head to the tips of your toes. Let warmth and kindness encircle you.

+++ Know that you can comfort yourself at any time by placing your hand over your heart and allowing compassion to soften and warm you.

In the space around the charger you might like to write or draw things that make you happy or bring you peace.

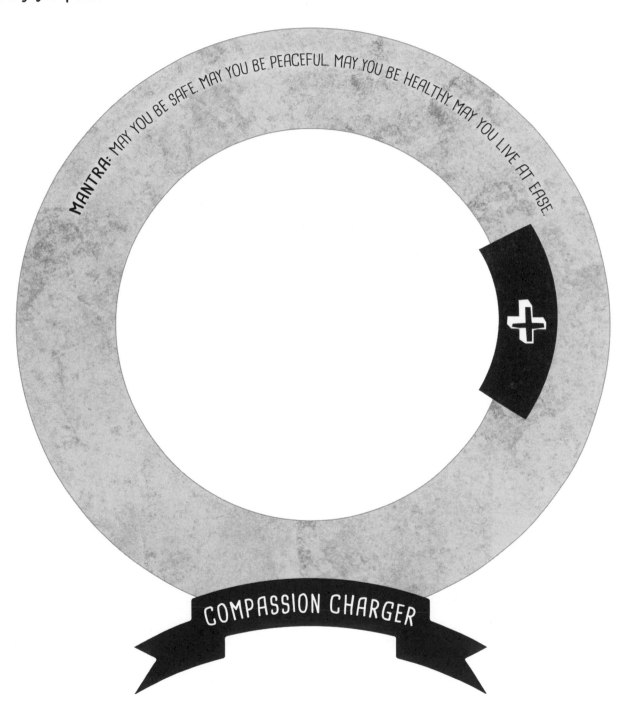

MANTRA: MAY YOU BE SAFE. MAY YOU BE PEACEFUL. MAY YOU BE HEALTHY. MAY YOU LIVE AT EASE.

COMPASSION CHARGER

INTERCONNECTION

 Remove the centre of the page opposite by cutting along the dotted lines. Looking carefully at this piece of paper, you can begin to see many things. You can see the trees that were used to make the paper, the rain that fell to water the trees, the clouds that turned into the rain, the oceans from which the clouds were formed. All of these things are in this piece of paper.

 You can also see all of the things this piece of paper might become. You might like to return the piece of paper to the natural world – release it to the wind, bury it, let it dissolve in water. It will biodegrade and its molecules will become part of something else. Perhaps it will return to the soil and become part of the body of an insect, then a bird flying through the clouds. Perhaps its carbon atoms will be used by a plant to make a beautiful sunflower.

 You can practise seeing the interconnectedness of everything around you at any time. For example, next time you drink a cup of tea you can contemplate the journey the water has taken to arrive in your mug: its journey through the oceans, through the bodies of many other beings, through rivers and clouds. You can become aware that as your body absorbs the water, it will become a part of you before it continues on its journey. Knowing that nothing around you will continue in its present form forever, you can appreciate the many miracles that exist in the present moment.

VIEWFINDER

Hold the page up and look through the viewfinder. (You can do this wherever you are right now.)

As you look, try not to label or define what you see but notice any shapes that are formed. Notice the way that lines and shapes interact. How many different colours can you see?

As you put down the viewfinder, smile with your eyes and feel them soften. Be aware of what a miracle it is that your eyes are able to see.

For the rest of the day, let your eyes drink in the view. Enjoy the colours and shapes. Feel your eyes caress the contours of the world around you.

SCROLL UP

Stand with your feet flat on the ground. Hold the book in both hands with your thumbs on the scroll buttons.

Scroll up and move both hands up as far as you can, arms straight, stretching the book above your head.

Focus your attention on the different muscle groups working within your body and on the sensation of moving through space.

Scroll down and bring the book down in front of you, bending at your knees if comfortable.

Let the movement flow. Repeat slowly and gracefully, allowing the movement to follow the breath.

Notice how your body feels after completing this exercise.

PAINT

Use the tools on this page to give shape to a thought or feeling that is present for you right now. Whatever image you choose to create is OK. You can enjoy seeing your creation in your mind as you draw.

When you have finished, take a moment to look at your image, zooming in and out as you wish.

When you turn the page, the screen will automatically clear.

Whenever a thought or image arises in your mind, you can invite it up and use this page to look at it clearly before allowing it to disperse and letting it go as you turn the page.

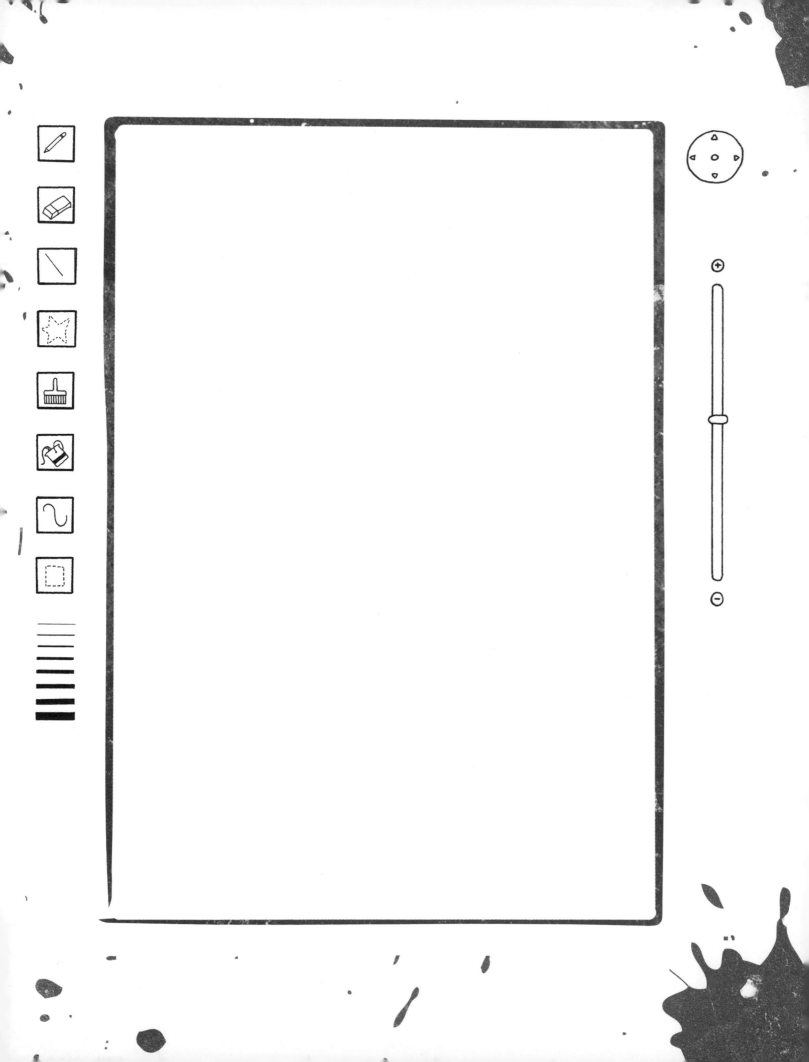

SCREEN CAPTURE

Go outside into the fresh air and look carefully at the plants around you.
Choose and pick five interestingly shaped leaves or flowers.

Place them on the page opposite until you are happy with your arrangement.
Now, select screen capture by closing this book and placing other books or
heavy objects on top for a day or two.

Take with you the sense of being able to carry with you the moments that
make you smile.

GRATITUDE

Take a slow breath and begin to notice sounds, sights and sensations in and around you as they are occurring in this present moment.

Now, try to bring to mind one thing that gives you a feeling of gladness and contentment. This may be something that is present right now or a happy memory. It might be the blue sky, the presence of a friend (human or animal), a flower that has just come into bloom or a heart-warming conversation you've had.

Next, click and hold the 'like' button in the picture opposite for ten seconds to allow this positive feeling to seep into and nourish your whole body. Notice a feeling of gladness flow through your fingers into your hands, arms, torso, legs, toes and heart: feel gratitude gently infuse and spread out as it fills your whole body.

Finally, lift your finger from the page and thank yourself for nurturing this positive feeling. Next time you notice something that you appreciate, you can come back to this page or simply put your hand on your chest and take a moment to really let the feeling land and settle in your body.

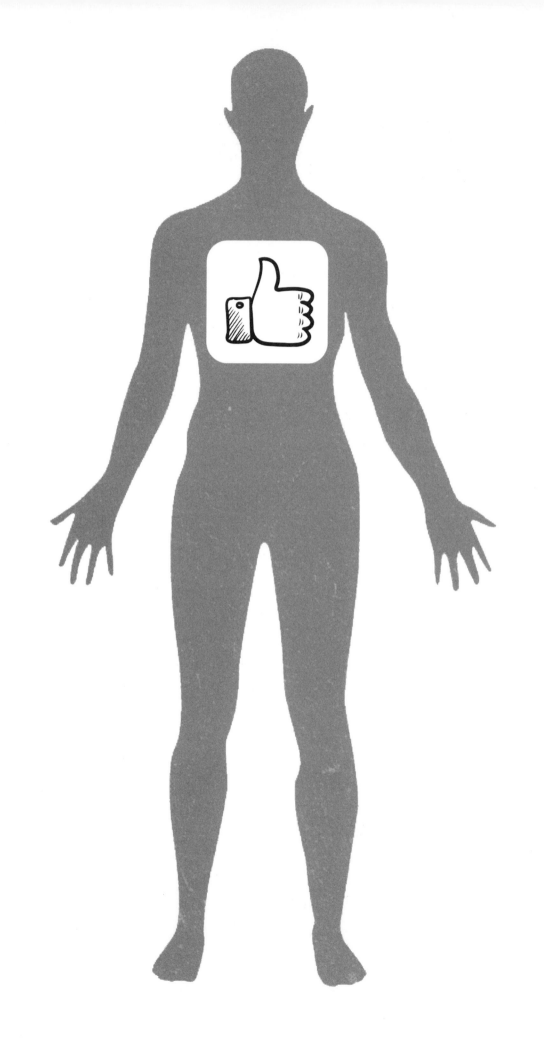

SCROLL DOWN

Begin by standing up and taking a slow breath.

Place your finger on the scroll button.

As you scroll down, your attention will move down through your body and then down through the different layers of the earth beneath your feet.

Begin to scroll down now, from the top of your head to the soles of your feet. Feel the touch of your feet on the ground. Move down through the soles of your feet and the floor, through the soil and the roots of plants. Descend further through the shifting plates of rock and down to where the rock becomes viscous and starts to flow. Finally, you will reach the very centre of the earth. The energy here is intense and vital. Stay for a moment visualising the purity of this white energy.

Now, slowly return up through the layers: the white centre, the magma flows, the shifting plates, the soil, the floor you are standing on and back up into the soles of your feet. Take a deep breath, stand firmly on the ground and feel your feet connect with the surface of the earth.

You can ease your busy mind at any time by moving your attention down into your feet or into the earth. Feel how your mind may rest when your attention is grounded.

THE PATH AHEAD

Looking at the picture on the page opposite, you can see that the ground is covered with debris and dead leaves. It is difficult to know where the path is or how to move forwards.

Take a deep, slow in-breath. Now, with a long and steady out-breath, blow across the page to scatter and clear the debris.

Now, turn the page.

THE PATH AHEAD

The steady force of your out-breath has cleared the debris and the path ahead can now be found.

In the same way, a slow, easeful breath can clear the mind.

With each breath, you may feel the breeze of fresh air cleansing your mind, illuminating the path ahead.

INWARD SMILE :)

Relax your face and feel a gentle half-smile on your lips. Breathing gently, relax the tiny muscles around your eyes and notice how it feels to smile with your eyes. Now, place your finger on the first circle. As you do so, become aware of the organ that is your brain and how it works so hard all the time to keep you alive. Imagine the smile flowing to your brain, bathing it in warm light. Take three calm breaths.

Repeat this for each of the inner organs pictured, including your heart, lungs, liver, kidneys, stomach and intestines. Smile and thank each organ for the hard work it does. Feel the relief as it releases all tension and is nourished by your appreciation and caring smile. Picture it bathed in a warm glow as it absorbs the light of your smile.

Notice how it feels when you appreciate your body and give it time to relax and feel at ease.

You will find that when your body is calm it is much easier for your mind to come back to rest in your body. When you feel your mind has run away, you can practise the inward smile and invite your mind to return peacefully to your body. You may notice a feeling of quiet confidence as your mind and body come back together.

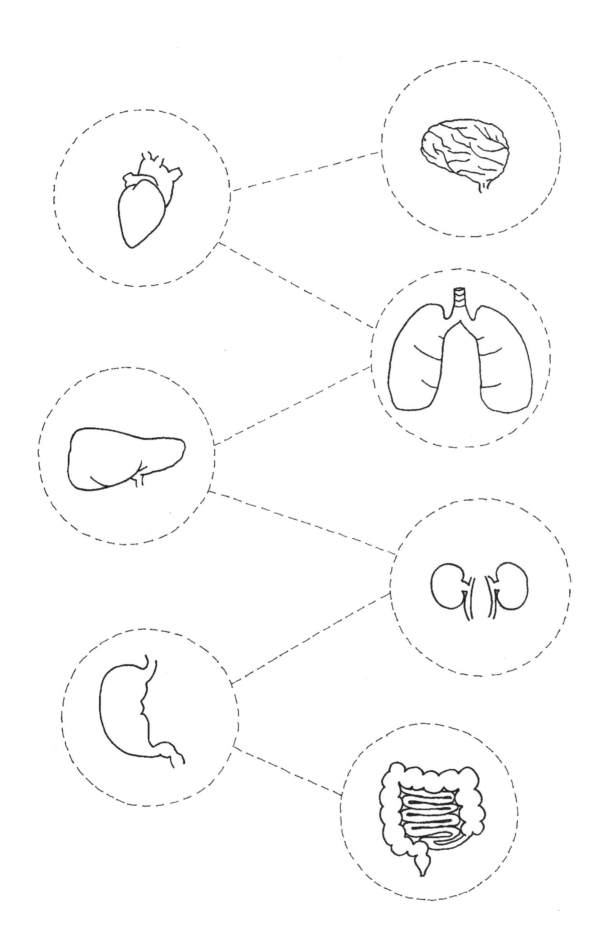

PROFILE PICTURE 👤

With your lips softly touching, begin to breathe gently through your nose. Take three slow breaths, saying to yourself, 'Now I am breathing in, now I am breathing out.' Notice the sensation of air moving into your nostrils as you breathe in and the sensation as it leaves your nostrils when you breathe out.

Now, let your eyes rest on the empty box on the page. You may relax your eyes as there is nothing to see or read upon the page. Simply allow your gaze to rest upon the empty box.

Become aware of the muscles in your face – your forehead, nose and cheeks, your chin, the small muscles around your mouth and the tiny muscles around your eyes. Breathe with a kindly awareness of the sensations in your face right now.

You may find that your tongue and face become tense in response to thoughts arising in your mind. That is OK. Every time you feel your muscles become tight or your jaw begin to clench, simply loosen and soften your face as you breathe. As your tongue loosens, your lips may part slightly.

When you are ready, turn away from the page and focus your eyes on the world around you again. Try to keep a softness in your face and a gentleness in your gaze. When you begin to feel tense, bring to mind the spaciousness of a blank page and allow all of the muscles in your face to let go and relax.

IMAGINE

This page will track the movement of your gaze. The plant that you choose to focus on will come to life and grow in your imagination. If you rest your attention gently and with a smile in your eyes, you may see it grow beautiful foliage and blossom to create wonderful shapes on the page. Only the plant that you choose to place your attention upon will flourish.

When you have nourished one seedling, you may wish to shift your attention to one of the other plants. That too will grow beautifully with its own leaf pattern and colour and its own unique shape. Notice the power of your attention and the infinite potential of your imagination.

AUDIO BALANCE

Use this page to balance your awareness between mind and body while listening to the radio or television.

Start with your finger on the middle button and begin to listen. Thoughts and feelings will arise associated with what you are hearing. Allow these to be present alongside an awareness of your breath and body.

If you feel you have become distracted and are no longer present with your body, slide your finger across to the body button. Become aware of any sensations in your body and breathe with them.

When you are ready, return to the space in between.

If you feel your awareness move too far from the words so that you are no longer able to follow what is being expressed, move your finger over to the other side and give your attention to the words and their meaning. Finally, come back to the middle space where you are able to be present with both your body and the words you hear.

Try to keep this balanced and spacious quality of listening with you throughout your day, whether you are reading, watching TV or talking to a friend.

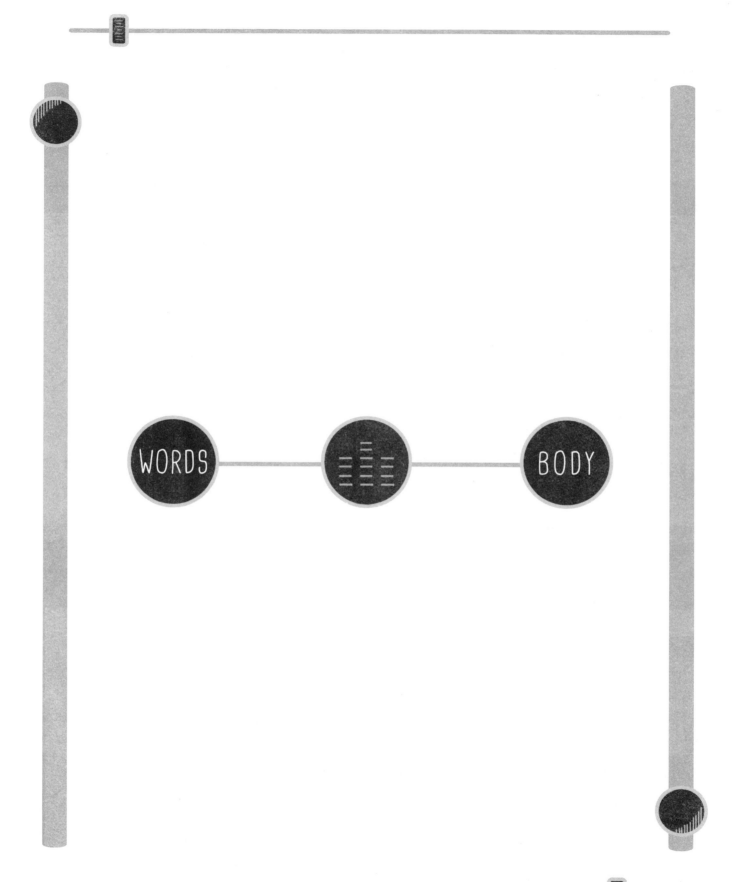

HOLD

Choose a set of opposites such as 'Dark + Light'. With your left thumb and forefinger, hold the bar on the left and say out loud the first word of each set, e.g. 'Dark'. Picture it and hold it in your mind. Now, take your right thumb and forefinger, hold the bar on the right and say out loud the second word, e.g. 'Light'. Again, picture it and hold it in your imagination.

Try to hold both opposites in your mind and now come back to your breath. Continue to breathe slowly, allowing both concepts equal space in your mind. There is no need to grasp onto the idea of one more than the other, but keep the image of both present in your imagination.

With a calm mind you will find yourself embracing both extremes and sensing the space in between opening up. This is a creative space where new ideas are formed.

As you become comfortable with this practice you can use your own set of opposites: it may be that you need to make a difficult decision between two things, or perhaps you are experiencing two opposing emotions such as pain and joy. Know that you have more than enough space to hold both. Breathe with the awareness of both and allow your mind to expand gently around them.

DARK + LIGHT
UP + DOWN
HAPPY + SAD
SKY + EARTH

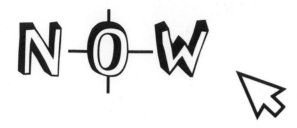

Where would you place 'now' on this timeline?

Place your finger on the spot that you would call 'now'.

Double-click this spot to bring yourself into the present moment. Notice the sound this movement makes. Feel the sensation of your fingertips touching the book.

'Now' can be found in any moment by becoming aware of all of the sights and sounds around you and the feelings and sensations you are experiencing in your mind and body.

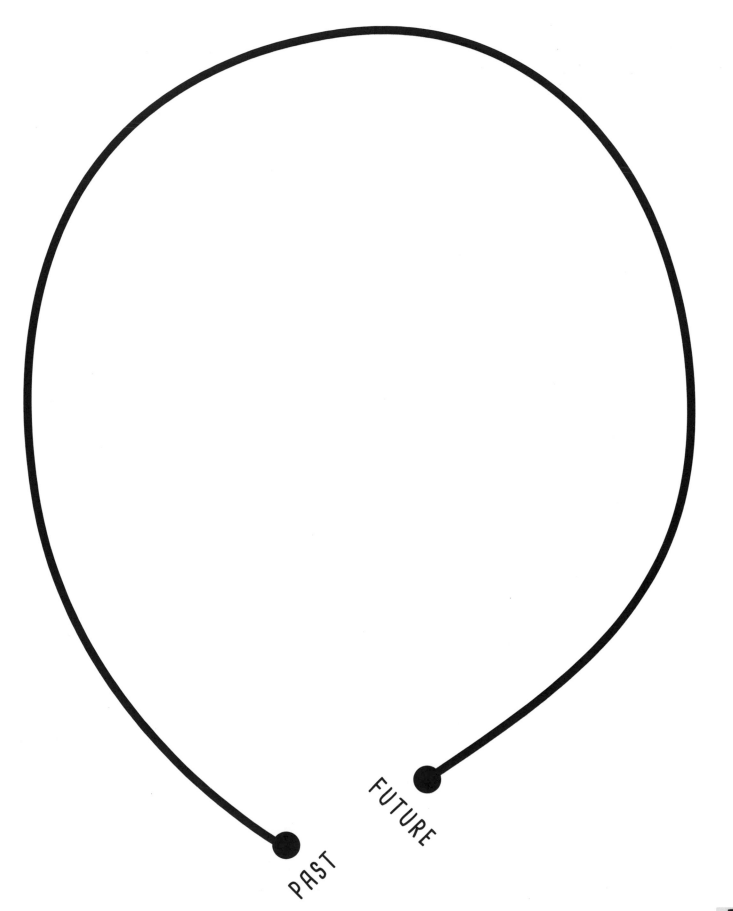

PAST

FUTURE

55

CONNECT

Take three slow breaths and feel your feet touching the floor or whatever surface they are resting upon.

Place your left forefinger in the left circle. Now, place your right forefinger in the right circle. This completes the circuit between you and the book. Feel the connection being made. Breathe slowly and with ease. As you breathe in, begin to sense energy moving up your left arm and warming your heart. As you breathe out, sense the energy flowing down through your right arm. As long as your fingers are touching the page this circuit of warming energy will continue to flow between you and the book. Feel it nourish and calm you.

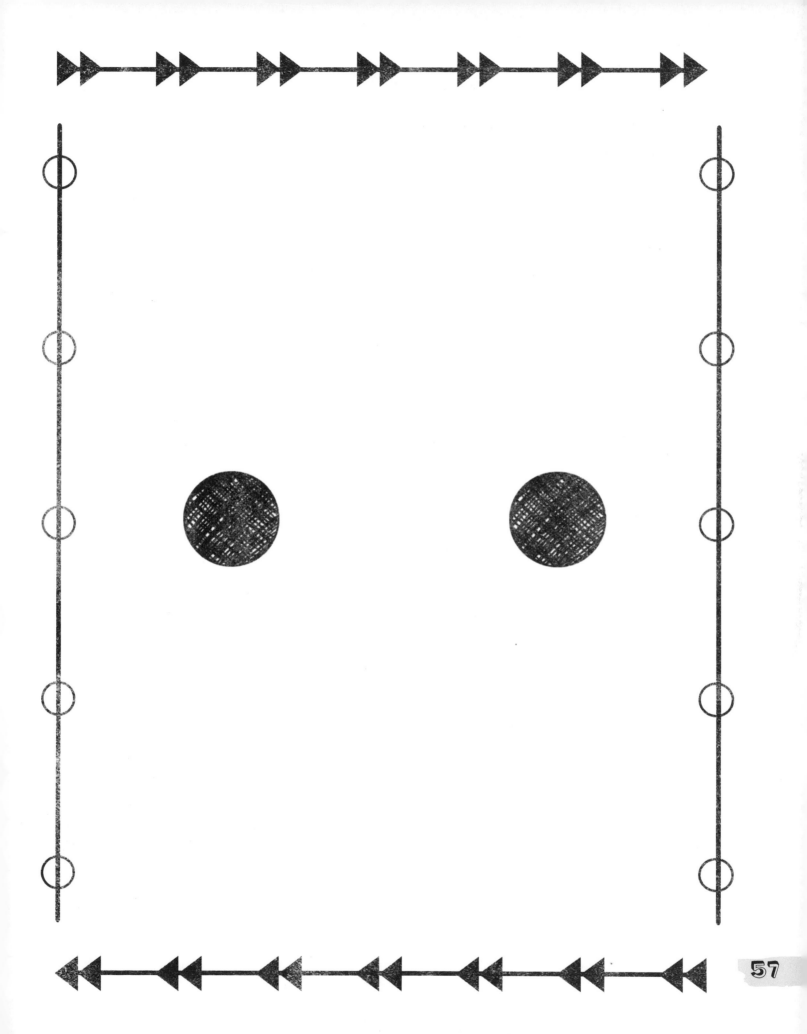

CONCLUSION

STEPPING INTO MINDFULNESS

The practices that you have tried in this book may slowly unfold within you and infuse through your mind and body gently over time. You can rest and let the ideas percolate as they will. Carry them with you and let them seep gradually into your day-to-day life.

Every moment of calm and compassion counts and will make it easier to come back to this place again in the future. In time, you may notice within you a softening and a growing sense of ease and balance: you may recognise more moments of peace and joy, and you may discover a deepening ability to be with whatever unfolds for you as you move through life.

You can come back to these activities at any time. They are here to support you, whatever you are feeling, in any moment.

You might like to consider ways in which you could bring these activities further into your daily life so that you can use them even when you do not have the book with you. Think about prompts or reminders you could make. Be creative! How about a sound button on a Post-it note? You could stick it somewhere that means you will see it regularly, such as the fridge. Every time you walk past you can take a moment to become aware of the sounds around you and the silences between sounds. Just a brief shift in attention like this can be very nourishing and make a big difference to the quality of your awareness as you move through the day.

DIFFERENT APPROACHES

CURIOSITY

Curiosity is a fun way with which to approach the world. We all have a tendency to slip into 'auto-pilot' and perceive what we expect to find rather than what is actually present around us. Many of the activities in this book encourage you to take time to notice what is really here. There is so much to discover! Be inspired by what is around you and be open to the spirit of enquiry. There is no need to reach a conclusion or formulate a perfect response. Simply open up your awareness and take an interest in all that you find.

LETTING GO

Your mind will always produce thoughts: it is what minds do. Thoughts may arise and then pass like clouds in the sky. Try not to hold onto each thought that arises in your mind – notice it and then let it go. Observe the flow of your thoughts as you might sit by a stream and watch with appreciation as the water flows over rocks and stones.

KINDNESS

We cannot be really present in the moment if we are holding on too tightly to the past or grasping onto our image of what the future might bring. Kindness soothes us and lets us rest with things just as they are. Let kindness surround your practice. Whatever arises is OK. There is no need to change your thoughts and feelings. Whenever you try one of these activities, be patient with yourself and give yourself time. Allow yourself to smile to your thoughts, feelings and perceptions, whatever they are. Simply by noticing them, you are doing all you need to do. There is no need to be anywhere else but where you are.

ACKNOWLEDGEMENTS AND USEFUL READING

I would like to thank my family and friends for their endless support and encouragement. I am very grateful to my friends at Wake Up for inspiring my own mindfulness practice. Many thanks to my agent Jennifer Christie from Graham Maw Christie for believing in this book and making it a fun project to work on, and Carolyn Thorne and her team at HarperCollins for all their work bringing it to life.

The activity 'A Moment to Pause' was inspired by the 'Mind Jar' in the book *Peaceful Piggy Meditation: An Introduction to Meditation for Children* by Kerry Lee MacLean.

The following books have informed and inspired many of the ideas behind the other activities:

Self-Compassion by Dr Kristin Neff, Professor of Psychology at the University of Texas.

Full Catastrophe Living by Dr Jon Kabat-Zinn, Professor of Medicine Emeritus and creator of the Stress Reduction Clinic and the Center for Mindfulness in Medicine, Health Care and Society at the University of Massachusetts Medical School.

Buddha's Brain: The Practical Neuroscience of Happiness, Love and Wisdom by Dr Rick Hanson, Psychologist and Senior Fellow of the Greater Good Science Center at the University of California, Berkeley.

All books by poet, activist and Zen master Thich Nhat Hanh, especially *No Death, No Fear, A Love Letter to the Earth* and *Reconciliation*.